OUR EARTH IN ACTION

RIVERS

Chris Oxlade

FRANKLIN WATTS

This edition published in 2014 by Franklin Watts

Copyright © 2014 Franklin Watts

Franklin Watts
338 Euston Road
London NW1 3BH

Franklin Watts Australia
Level 17/207 Kent Street
Sydney, NSW 2000

A CIP catalogue record for this book is available
from the British Library.

Dewey number: 551.48' 3

ISBN 978 1 4451 3196 2

Printed in China

Franklin Watts is a division of Hachette Children's Books,
an Hachette UK company.
www.hachette.co.uk

Artwork: John Alston
Editor: Sarah Ridley
Design: Thomas Keenes
Editor in Chief: John C. Miles
Art director: Jonathan Hair
Picture Research: Diana Morris

Picture credits: Lin Alder/Alamy: 29. Xiaobo Chen/Alamy: 22. Ashley Cooper/Alamy: 14b.
Stewart Drolet/istockphoto: 25. Nemanja Glumac/istockphoto: 28. Greenshoots
International/Alamy: 15. Wolfgang Kaehler/Alamy: 27. Istvan Daniel Kiraly/istockphoto: 20.
Scott Leman/istockphoto: 14t. Jonathan Ling/istockphoto: 18-19. Yenwen Lu/istockphoto: 7.
NASA: 12. T Ness/istockphoto: 9.Johannes Norpoth/istockphoto: 21. John
Novis/Photofusion/Alamy: 23. Dave Porter/Alamy: 10-11. Sandsun/istockphoto: 8. Philip
Scalia/Alamy: 16-17.Kevin Schafer/Alamy: 6. Colin Shepherd/Rex Features: 16t.Sipa
Press/Rex Features: 19t. Wonganan Sukcharoenkana/istockphoto: 11b. Milan
Tesar/Shutterstock: front cover, 1. TT/istockphoto: 4-5.John Phillip Young/istockphoto: 13.
*Every attempt has been made to clear copyright. Should there be any inadvertent
omission please apply to the publisher for rectification.*

CONTENTS

ABOUT RIVERS 4

RIVERS AND LANDSCAPES 6

UPPER RIVER STAGES 8

MIDDLE RIVER STAGES 10

LOWER RIVER STAGES 12

RIVER SCIENCE 14

FLOODS 16

FLOOD PROTECTION 18

RIVER RESOURCES 20

DAMS 22

CASE STUDY: THE MISSISSIPPI 24

CASE STUDY: THE NILE 26

RIVER PROBLEMS 28

GLOSSARY 30

FURTHER INFORMATION 31

INDEX 32

ABOUT RIVERS

A river is a channel in the ground that water flows along. Rivers drain the land close to them. They carry water from rainfall, from melting snow, and from under the ground to the sea.

Rivers shape the Earth's surface, creating landforms. They are a vital resource for us all — for water supply, irrigation, industry, transport and energy.

RIVER SYSTEMS

We normally think of a river as a single channel of water but nearly all rivers are part of a river system. The place where a river starts is called its source. Here, even the greatest rivers may begin life as a trickle of water. Pulled by gravity, the water flows downstream. Soon other streams join the river, adding water and making it larger. It becomes a small river, which is joined by other small rivers. These other rivers are called tributaries. The river continues to grow as it flows towards the sea. The area of land drained by a river and its tributaries is called a drainage basin. The high ground between the drainage basins of different rivers is called a watershed.

THE WATER CYCLE

The flow of water down rivers is part of the water cycle. This is the constant movement of water between the oceans, the atmosphere and the land. Freshwater starts as rain and other precipitation that falls from the atmosphere. It makes its way back to the sea, carried along in streams and rivers. Seawater evaporates to form water vapour in the atmosphere, which condenses to make rain clouds and the cycle begins again.

CHANGING THE LANDSCAPE

Rivers change the landscape as they flow across it. They erode (wear away) rocks and soil in some places, cutting valleys in hills and mountains. The eroded material is washed downstream. It builds up the landscape where the material is deposited. Dramatic changes can happen when large rivers are in flood.

water falls as rain and snow

water stored as ice

condensation forms clouds

water vapour released from plants

water evaporates from lakes

sea

water evaporates from sea

rivers

water stored in lakes

underground channel

runoff from land

▲ *A diagram of the water cycle. Rivers carry water that runs off the land back to the sea.*

◀ *This river has cut its way through the landscape, creating the valley through which it flows.*

How much water?

Two-thirds of the Earth's surface are covered with water. Almost all of it (about 97.5%) is saltwater in the oceans and seas. Of the 2.5% that is freshwater, two-thirds are locked up in ice caps. Almost all the rest is in soil and rocks. Less than 1% of the world's freshwater is in rivers and lakes.

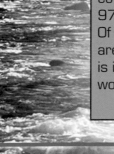

RIVERS AND LANDSCAPES

Flowing water is one of the major forces that shapes the Earth's surface. It helps to erode hills and mountains, wearing them away and levelling the surface. Rivers erode by breaking up rocks and carrying them away. The rocky material, called sediment, is deposited downstream. Together, erosion and deposition are responsible for the shape of rivers and various landscapes.

BREAKING ROCKS

So how do rivers erode solid rocks? Firstly, by the action of the river water itself, which pushes and pulls on rocks in a river's bed and banks as it swirls around. This is called hydraulic action. Then the bits of rock cause erosion themselves. They break up more rock because they smash down on the river-bed as they are carried along by the water. The rocks also hit against each other in the water, which wears them down into rounded boulders or pebbles. This process is called attrition. The faster and more turbulent the water, the more it erodes the river channel.

TRANSPORTATION

Once loose pieces of rock (sediment) are in the water, they are carried downstream by it. The moving sediment is called the load, and the movement of it is called transportation. Small pieces of sediment are carried in the water. While the water is turbulent, these particles

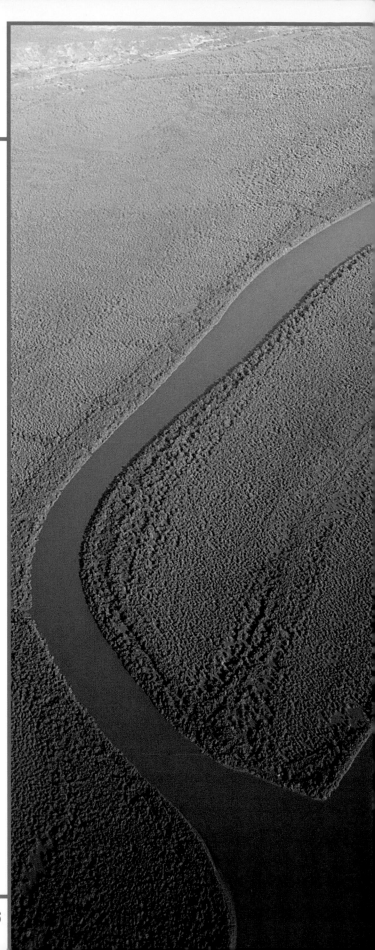

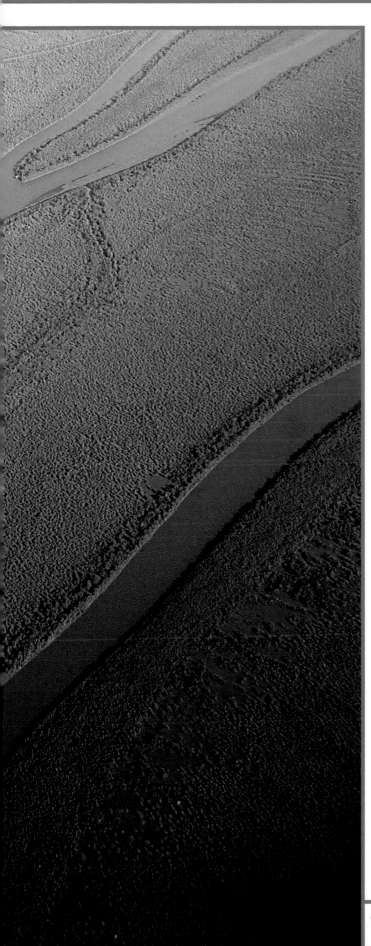

Chemical weathering

The chemicals that make up some rocks are changed by water, and this can break the rocks up. This process is called chemical weathering. A common example is weathering of limestone rock, which slowly dissolves in the water that flows over it. This can erode underground passageways and caves that rivers flow through.

▼ *A cave created by chemical weathering.*

◄ *The water in this river is coloured brown by the load of sediment it is carrying.*

don't settle. Nor do the larger particles, which bump along the river-bed. During floods, even large boulders can be transported in this way.

DEPOSITION
Where a river flows slowly and smoothly, without too much turbulence, the load it carries settles to the river-bed. This is called deposition, and it builds up layers of sediment. Deposition happens at river bends, at a river's mouth, and on land next to the river during floods.

UPPER RIVER STAGES

Rivers flow downhill from hills and mountains, through valleys and across plains. Hydrologists often divide a river's route into three stages — upper, middle and lower (or young, middle-aged and old). At each stage a river has a different character and creates different landforms. Here we look at the upper stages of a river.

SOURCES OF WATER

All rivers start at a place called a source. Here there is a flow of water that forms the upper stages of a river. A common river source is a spring, where water from underground emerges at the surface. Springs are normally at the base of a hill. Other sources of water for rivers include lakes and, in spring, melting ice and snow. When it is raining, water runs off fields into rivers, and also seeps underground, making springs flow more quickly. All this water feeds small streams, which join each other to form rivers.

▼ In mountainous areas of the world, rivers are fed by melting ice and snow.

UPPER RIVER FLOW

Because rivers start life in hills and mountains, they begin by flowing down steep slopes. The water flow is normally turbulent (rough and random, rather than smooth), because it tumbles over rocks and boulders and down waterfalls. The water might look fast because of the turbulence, but on average, this is where rivers flow at their slowest.

UPPER RIVER LANDFORMS

In its upper stages, a river cuts steep-sided valleys in the landscape. These valleys are called V-shaped valleys because in cross-section they look like a letter 'V'. The river flows along the bottom of the valley, and slowly erodes downwards through the rocks. Rocks and soil slide into the river from the valley sides. All this material is carried downstream by the river.

▲ *The upper stage of a river, flowing steeply over bare rocks.*

Waterfalls

High waterfalls form where there are two different types of rock under a river. When a river flows over hard rock then over soft rock, the soft rock erodes more quickly than the hard rock. The soft rock wears away, leaving a step that the river flows over. The falling water continues to erode the soft rock, creating a pool at the base of the waterfall.

MIDDLE RIVER STAGES

As a river moves out of the hills where it starts, it begins to flow over less steep ground, and changes character. The river becomes wider and deeper, and its flow becomes less turbulent and smoother. It develops large bends and erodes wide valleys on its way to the sea.

MEANDERS

Rivers naturally bend from side to side. These bends are called meanders. In the middle stages of a river the meanders become longer, and some rivers snake dramatically, swinging one way and then the other across the landscape. Meanders form because water flows more quickly on the outside of bends than on the inside. This causes more erosion on the outside of a bend, which eats away the river bank. The inside of the bend is built up by sediment. Over the years, the meanders get wider and sharper.

VALLEYS AND FLOOD PLAINS

Over many years, the changing meanders of a river erode a valley. The outsides of a river's bends cut into the valley sides, making the valley wider. These valleys tend to be wide, with gentle hills on each side,

▼ A river meandering across the flat flood plain of its valley.

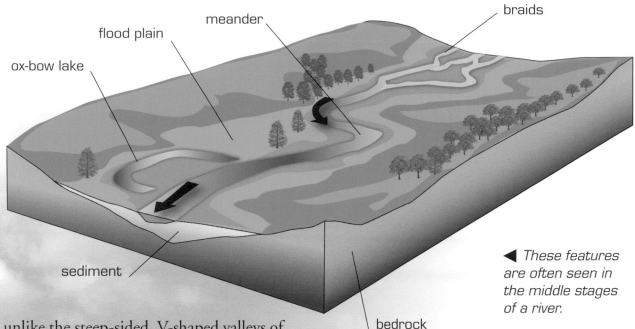

ox-bow lake

flood plain

meander

braids

sediment

bedrock

◀ These features are often seen in the middle stages of a river.

unlike the steep-sided, V-shaped valleys of upper river stages on pages 8-9. When a river floods, water overflows its banks, carrying sediment across its valley. The sediment builds up in layers in the valley bottom, forming flat land on either side of the river. These areas of land are called flood plains. The material on a flood plain is constantly eroded and deposited as a river's meanders change shape.

Ox-bow lakes

As a river's meanders slowly migrate across a flood plain, two meanders, one downstream from the other, can move towards each other. Eventually they meet, and the river flows between them. This often happens during a flood, when erosion is at its greatest. The river settles into its new channel, leaving a horseshoe-shaped section of the old river cut off. This section is known as an ox-bow lake. It slowly dries up and fills in with sediment.

▼ Over time, the bend in this river will become an ox-bow lake.

LOWER RIVER STAGES

By the time a river approaches the sea, many tributaries have joined it, and it is wide, deep and fast-flowing. It meanders across the coastal plain, the flat land near the coast, and then flows into the sea. At the river's mouth, freshwater from the river and saltwater from the sea mix together.

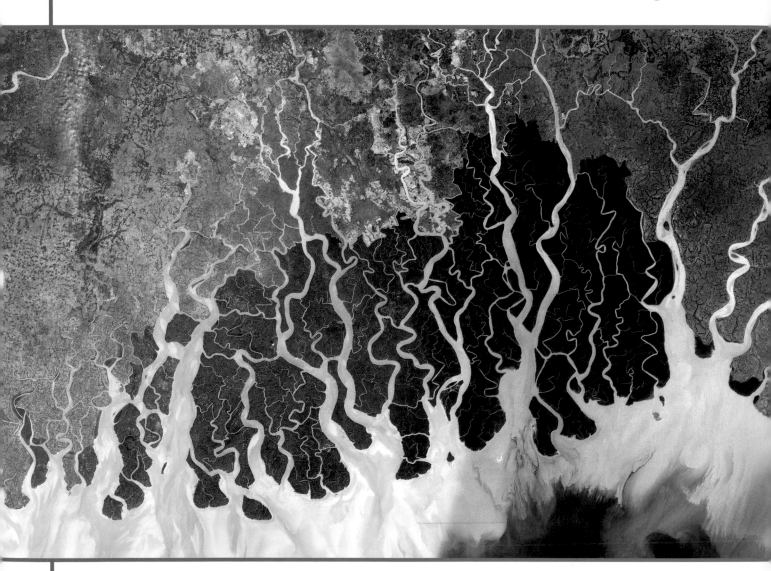

DELTAS

When a river flows into the sea, its water slows down. The sediment that it has carried downstream is deposited in layers on the sea-bed. Large particles, such as pebbles, are dropped first while very fine sediment can be carried far out to sea. Some rivers carry large amounts of sediment because they have eroded soft rocks quickly. Where these

▲ *The complex channels of the Ganges delta, seen from space.*

Where a river flows across a low-lying coastal plain or a delta before it enters the sea, the lower part of the river is tidal. This means that at high tide, seawater pushes the river's water back upstream, and the river level rises twice a day. This can affect the river level many kilometres inland, although its effect becomes harder to detect.

▼ *The tidal section of a river close to the sea.*

rivers flow into shallow seas the sediment builds up until it breaks the surface, forming new land at the river mouth. This land is called a delta, and as long as sediment comes down the river, the delta grows. The river flows across the delta to the sea beyond, often splitting into different channels, called distributaries. The channels often change position during floods. Deltas come in different shapes. Two common shapes are the fan-shaped delta and the bird's-foot delta.

ESTUARIES

An estuary is a river mouth where the coastline bends inland. A river flows into the top end of the estuary. At high tide the sea fills the estuary. As the tide falls, mud flats are revealed, which are made up of sediment from the river. The river flows across the mud in channels and into the sea at the mouth of the estuary. It may meander through the mud. There are often salt marshes along the edges of an estuary, which are flooded during very high tides. The plants that grow in salt marshes have adapted to live in salty conditions that would kill most plants.

RIVER SCIENCE

The science of rivers is part of the science of hydrology, which is the study of water in the environment. Hydrologists study how water moves around the water cycle, river flow, river basins and water quality. They try to find solutions to problems such as floods and water shortages.

MEASURING RIVER FLOW

The amount of water flowing down a river is called its discharge. This is the volume of water that flows past a place on the river in a certain period of time. It is usually measured in cubic metres per second. To calculate discharge, hydrologists need to know the depth of water in the river and the speed of the flow. These measurements are taken with an instrument called a stream gauge. Many rivers have permanent stream gauges at various places along their banks. They are read manually, or send data to a central collection point remotely.

▲ A stream gauge shows the depth of water in a river.

USING DISCHARGE MEASUREMENTS

Many large river systems have a network of stream gauges on the main river and its major tributaries. Measurements from these show how water is draining from a river basin. Studying records from the past allows hydrologists to understand how water drains when there is rain in one part of a basin or another, and to build computer models of a basin. These models can predict how river levels will rise and fall due to

Tracing a flow

Some rivers travel underground for part of their course. They disappear down sink holes in one place and emerge downstream, possibly many kilometres away. Hydrologists may want to find out how different tributaries are connected underground. They put bright dye into the river upstream of the sink hole and watch to see where the dye emerges.

▶ An hydrologist adds dye to an icy river to trace its path.

certain rain patterns. This is especially important in flood prediction (see pages 16-17).

WATER QUALITY

Hydrologists collect samples of river water to measure the level of different materials and chemicals in it. They might be interested in the sediment, to see how much is being carried downstream. Some hydrologists will be interested in the health of the river, and so they will measure levels of pollutants and micro-organisms.

▲ *Hydrologists taking water samples to test the health of a river. This monitoring is vital to help prevent danger to people or the environment.*

FLOODS

A flood happens when the water level in a river rises above the level of its banks. The water spills out across the river's flood plains. Floods happen after long periods of rain in all or part of a river's drainage basin. The ground becomes saturated, and further rain has nowhere to go but into rivers.

FLOOD PATTERNS

If more water pours into a river than the river can carry away, the river's level rises. Eventually the river overflows from its channel and causes a flood. When the rain stops, the level begins to fall again. A surge of water moves downstream. As it passes a point on the river, the water level rises and then falls again. In large river basins, the surge can cause flooding far

Flash floods

Flash floods happen when extremely heavy rain falls in a small area. They are often caused by thunderstorms. Streams and small rivers fill rapidly with water and overflow. Most damage is caused by debris-filled torrents of water. People can be swept away by flash floods.

▼ A flash flood in Boscastle, England, in 2004.

far downstream from where the rain fell, and sometimes days after the rain has stopped.

On most rivers, flooding is more likely at certain times of the year, when more rainfall comes down, or when water enters the rivers from melting winter snow. There can be twenty times more water being carried along a river in a wet season than a dry season.

FLOOD EFFECTS

In the upper stages of a river, floods lead to increased erosion, and a heavier load of sediment in the river. In the middle and lower stages of the river, water spreads over flood plains and deposits the sediment. Increased erosion here can change the course of the river by breaking through between meanders, creating ox-bow lakes (see page 11).

FLOOD DAMAGE

Floods cause damage to property in two ways. Firstly, the force of flowing water can knock down structures, and erosion can rip up road surfaces and undermine foundations. Secondly, water seeps into properties, filling the lower floors and ruining fixtures, fittings, decorations and furniture. Outdoors, cars are submerged or washed away. Crops growing on flood plains can be ruined. The flood water can force sewage from drains, contaminating water supplies.

▼ *The Mohawk river in New York State has a history of flooding. Particularly bad floods, in 2006 (shown here) and in 2011, damaged the huge barge locks, one of which is shown here.*

FLOOD PROTECTION

Millions of people live on flood plains. There are many good reasons for living there — the land is flat and fertile and so perfect for farming, and the river provides a water supply and a convenient transport system. In many countries people have nowhere else to live because of a shortage of land. So how do they protect themselves against floods?

FLOOD PROTECTION METHODS

The simplest flood protection method is to build walls (often called levees) on the river banks, so that the water level in the river can rise higher without flooding. These walls are normally simple earth embankments. Other methods rely on changing the route of the river. Straightening a river's path allows the water to flow down it faster, and so reduce the chance of flooding. Diversion channels and flood pools take water from the river and store it until the flood water has passed. Dams prevent flooding by catching flood water and releasing it slowly downstream. On tidal rivers, tidal barriers stop very high tides from reaching up the river and causing floods in populated areas.

▼ The Thames Barrier helps protect London, England, from floods. It closes to prevent very high tides moving up the River Thames and flooding the city.

The flood protection debate

There is an ongoing debate about whether flood protection is a good idea or not. Reasons for flood protection include preventing loss of property, with its huge cost and inconvenience, and the fact that it allows us to use flood plains for building. But some experts argue that flood protection stops natural flood patterns, which replenish farming land, and can also make flooding downstream of the protection worse. They also argue that if a levee or dam should fail, flooding would be much worse than if there were no protection at all.

◀ Flood defences in New Orleans, USA.

FLOOD WARNING SYSTEMS

Hydrologists use computer models of river drainage basins to try to predict floods. They feed in data about rainfall in the basin and stream gauge readings, and the models calculate the chances of flooding at places along the river. They issue warnings to local authorities and the public. Flash floods are hard to predict as it is difficult for weather forecasters to say exactly where torrential rain is going to fall.

RIVER RESOURCES

Rivers are important resources for us. So what do we use them for? They are sources of water and food, they are transport routes, places for leisure, and sources of energy (see page 22). This is why so many towns and cities have grown up alongside rivers for thousands of years.

USING RIVER WATER

Water is extracted from rivers for domestic use (drinking, showering, washing and so on), irrigation (watering crops) and for use by industries. Domestic water is cleaned to remove dirt and micro-organisms before it is distributed to homes and businesses. After use, water is cleaned at water treatment works before being released back into rivers. Cleaning is important as the same water may be extracted and used again at a place further downstream. In rural areas, water is pumped from rivers straight onto fields for watering crops. In some parts of the world, annual floods (see page 17) are vital for filling paddy fields with water to grow rice.

▲ *These paddy fields in China are filled with water from the nearby river.*

RIVER TRANSPORT

Large rivers are an efficient way of moving cargo between factories and ports. Bulk cargo, such as coal, iron ore and grain, is particularly suited to transport by ship. Ocean-going ships can reach inland ports along rivers, and many of the world's major ports are far inland. In remote areas, where there are few roads, rivers are a vital transport link for people, too. But few rivers are naturally navigable for their entire length. Waterfalls, rapids or shallows block the path of boats, and engineering is needed to by-pass them. Weirs divide the rivers into level sections, and locks allow boats to move up and down between one section and the next. Many river transport routes use both rivers and canals, with the level of water in the canals kept topped up by river water.

Living by rivers

People like to live by rivers because river banks are usually pleasant places to be. They offer views of the river, fishing, boating and walking. Riverside properties are often more expensive to buy than other properties. However, properties close to rivers are more at risk from floods.

▼ *The River Rhine links many cities in northern Europe. This container-carrying barge is at Düsseldorf in Germany.*

DAMS

A dam is a wall built across a river to trap river water. The water forms a lake called a reservoir behind the dam. People build dams to collect water for water supply and for irrigation, to control floods and to produce hydroelectricity. Some large rivers have a whole series of dams and reservoirs on them. Dams solve some problems but create others.

DAM BUILDING

A dam can only be built in a valley, as the sides of the valley contain the reservoir. The rocks at the site must be suitable too — some rocks are porous and would allow reservoir water to seep away or flow under the dam. There are several types of dam. Long, low dams are made from rock and earth, and called embankment dams. Narrow, tall concrete

Dam problems

Building a dam on a river changes how the water in the river has flowed naturally for thousands or millions of years. A dam stops the river flow until the reservoir is full, then only spare water is released. It prevents floods from happening downstream, and stops the movement of sediment down the river. This changes how the river erodes and deposits sediment. A reservoir floods the valley upstream of the dam, which drowns animal habitats, towns and villages. In general, small and micro-hydroelectric projects do not create these problems.

▼ *Part of the Three Gorges Dam in China, which flooded the scenic Three Gorges Valley.*

arch dams are built in canyons, where the water in the reservoir will be very deep. Other types of dam are the gravity dam and buttress dam, which are both heavy concrete walls.

ELECTRICITY FROM WATER

River water has energy because it flows downhill. A hydroelectric dam traps water, making a deep reservoir. The water is allowed to flow from the reservoir down pipes to the hydroelectric generating station below the dam. Here it spins turbines. The turbines operate generators that make electricity. The largest dams generate enough electricity for entire cities but not all hydroelectricity is made at large dams. Small and micro-hydroelectric stations work on a supply of water diverted from a river. They make electricity for individual homes, factories or small communities.

▶ *The tidal barrage on the River Rance in France. It produces electricity as the tide rises and falls.*

CASE STUDY: THE MISSISSIPPI

With a total length of 3,766 km, the Mississippi is the second longest river in North America (after the Missouri, one of its tributaries). Its drainage basin is the third largest in the world, covering 41% of mainland USA. Water takes about three months to flow along its length, supplying cities and industries, and forming a vital transport system.

▲ A location map of the Mississippi in the USA.

MISSISSIPPI RESOURCES

The Mississippi is one of the USA's major trade routes. Hundreds of weirs and locks, built and maintained by the US Army Corps of Engineers, allow giant barges to travel thousands of kilometres from Minneapolis in the north to New Orleans on the Gulf Coast. Barges visit at any of the dozens of cities in between. The route is especially important for wheat farmers on the plains of middle America. Two-thirds of the wheat harvest is carried by barge down the Mississippi to be exported from ports on the coast. The Mississippi also supplies water and drainage for homes, industries and the thousands of farms along its river banks.

▶ The Mississippi flows through St Louis, Missouri, USA. The Missouri joins the Mississippi just north of St Louis.

FLOWS AND FLOODS

On average over a year, 18,100 m³ of water (that's enough to fill five Olympic swimming pools) flows from the Mississippi's mouth into the Gulf of Mexico every second. The flow is much higher in the spring and early summer when water from melting snow in the Rocky Mountains combines with water from summer rains on the plains. This is when the flood risk is at its highest. The Mississippi has hundreds of kilometres of levees along its banks, as well as floodways built to divert water to other rivers. However, there have been major floods on the Mississippi. In 2005, New Orleans was flooded when a storm surge from Hurricane Katrina moved up the river, and the levees collapsed.

The Mississippi delta

The Mississippi carries a vast amount of sediment downstream and dumps it into the Gulf of Mexico, forming a delta. Geological evidence shows the delta has spread 80 km out to sea over the last 5,000 years. It is a vast area of low-lying salt marshes, swamps, lakes and mud flats, cut through by numerous river channels.

CASE STUDY: THE NILE

The River Nile is the world's longest river. If flows 6,650 km northwards across Africa. It is a hugely important river to millions of people in several different countries. As it is the only source of water for many, and allows crops to be grown in desert areas, it has caused tensions between countries. It is also a vital transport link and a source of power.

▲ A location map of the River Nile in Africa.

THE NILE'S COURSE

The source of the River Nile lies in mountains in the country of Rwanda. This is in the tropics, where the river is fed by heavy rains. The northern section of the river flows through the countries of Sudan and Egypt, across the Nubian Desert. Its mouth is on the Mediterranean Sea. The Nile has two major tributaries – the White Nile, which is the main river, and the Blue Nile.

THE NILE AND AGRICULTURE

The Nile has been an important river for thousands of years. The civilisation of ancient Egypt could not have grown without it. The river allowed the Egyptians to survive and thrive in this desert area. The Egyptians relied on annual floods to supply new minerals to their fields (but the floods also caused disasters). They cultivated a narrow strip of land along each river bank. The same land is farmed today. The green fields form a wide green stripe across the brown desert.

THE NILE DELTA

Over millions of years sediment carried down the Nile has created a 240-km-wide, fan-shaped delta on the Mediterranean coast. The river breaks into two distributaries on the delta. The delta land is used mainly for agriculture, but there are cities here too, including the port of Alexandria.

▶ Nile water allows a narrow strip of land to be farmed between the river and the desert.

The Aswan Dam

The Aswan Dam was completed on the Nile in 1971, creating Lake Nasser. It was built to overcome the problems of low water levels at certain times of the year — which led to lack of water for irrigation, to protect against floods, and to produce hydroelectricity. Unfortunately, the dam has caused problems downstream. There are no longer floods to replenish the fields with sediment, and farmers must now use artificial fertilisers. Sediment no longer reaches the delta either, and this has started to erode away the coast. Fishing stocks in the Mediterranean around the delta have suffered because of the lack of nutrients coming down the river.

RIVER PROBLEMS

We have seen examples in this book of how human activities cause problems by changing the natural flow of rivers. Dam building and flood protection can cause problems as well as solve them. Industry and agriculture also affect the river water, making it unhealthy.

POLLUTION

Many rivers suffer from pollution. Sources of pollution include untreated sewage, industrial effluent, general rubbish and fertilisers washed in from fields. Pollution affects animals and plants that live in rivers, and makes river water unsafe to drink. Fertilisers cause plants such as algae to grow quickly in rivers. The plants clog up the river and reduce oxygen levels in the water, making it difficult for fish and other aquatic animals to survive. However, many rivers that used to be badly polluted and lifeless have now been cleaned up.

▼ *Typical waste in a polluted river. These plastics will stay in the river for many years.*

OVER-EXTRACTION

Population growth and industrial development mean that more water is needed every year. Over-extraction of water from rivers has become a major problem. One example is the Colorado River in western USA. Twenty-five million people use its water. So much is extracted for irrigation in the desert and for cities such as Las Vegas, that today hardly any water reaches the sea at the Colorado's mouth. Where the people of different countries rely on the same river, over-extraction by one country can lead to political tension.

▲ *Over-extraction of water in the Colorado River, USA, means that the river-bed often dries out.*

LOOKING AFTER RIVERS

Access to freshwater is one of the world's major issues, and much of the water we need comes from rivers. Rivers are vital for the environments along their banks. In the past we have damaged some rivers badly. But our experience of river management is improving. We must take care of our rivers, allow them to flow and keep them clean.

The dry sea

The Aral Sea lies on the border between Kazakhstan and Uzbekistan. In the 1960s this inland sea began to shrink as water from the rivers that fed it was diverted for cotton growing in the former USSR. By the year 2000 the Aral Sea was just a quarter of its original size. It was a disaster for the families who lived around its shore. Today, however, the situation is being slowly reversed. A dam across the lake and the removal of dams on the rivers has allowed part of the lake to begin filling again.

GLOSSARY

atmosphere the layer of air that surrounds the Earth

dam a wall across a river that stops water flowing downstream

delta an area of low-lying land where a river meets the sea, formed by sediment carried down the river

deposition the dropping of sediment by a river

downstream further down a river, towards the sea

drainage basin the area of land drained by a river and its tributaries

erosion the wearing away of the landscape

fertiliser material put onto crops that contains nutrients that the crops need to grow

flood plain flat land alongside a river that is covered with water during a flood

hydraulic to do with liquids

hydrologist a scientist who studies water in the environment

ice cap a very thick (many kilometres in some places) sheet of ice covering some cold parts of the Earth

meanders a series of wide bends in a river across its flood plain

micro-organisms living things that are too small to see with the naked eye

mouth the place where a river flows into the sea

nutrients chemicals that plants and animals need to take in to grow and live

ox-bow lake a curved lake left when a river breaks through between two meanders

reservoir a lake formed by water trapped behind a dam

saturated describes something that is so wet that it cannot soak up any more water

sediment small particles of rock carried by a river and deposited downstream

sink hole a hole in the rock where a river flowing across the surface disappears underground

source the place where a river starts

spring a place where water emerges from underground

tide the rise and fall of the sea level, caused mainly by the gravity of the Moon

transportation the movement of rocky material along a river

tributary a river that feeds water into a larger river

turbulent describes a liquid that does not flow smoothly, but in a rough and random way

upstream further up a river, towards its source

weathering the breaking up of rocks into smaller particles

Further information

BBC Learning Zone clips
A short video where the presenter visits an ox-bow lake and explains how it formed.
www.bbc.co.uk/learningzone/clips/rivers-oxbow-lakes/405.html

NASA
A catalogue of visible Earth images from NASA. This page includes images of many huge deltas.
http://visibleearth.nasa.gov/view_cat.php?categoryID=785

UK Environment Agency
A page on floods, flood warnings and flood advice.
http://www.environment-agency.gov.uk/homeandleisure/floods/default.aspx

United States Geological Survey
The part of the website dedicated to water as a resource.
www.usgs.gov/water/

Another site developed by the US Geological Survey explains how hydroelectricity works.
http://water.usgs.gov/edu/hyhowworks.html

United States National Park Service
Information on the science and nature of the Mississippi.
www.nps.gov/miss/naturescience/index.htm

University of California
An animated water cycle diagram from the University of California.
http://earthguide.ucsd.edu/earthguide/diagrams/watercycle/

NOTE TO PARENTS AND TEACHERS:
Every effort has been made by the Publishers to ensure that the websites in this book are suitable for children, that they are of the highest educational value, and that they contain no inappropriate or offensive material. However, because of the nature of the Internet, it is impossible to guarantee that the contents of these sites will not be altered. We strongly advise that Internet access is supervised by a responsible adult.

INDEX

action, hydraulic 6
agriculture 18, 19, 24, 26 28
Aral Sea 29
attrition 6

barrages, tidal 23
barriers, tidal 18
basins, drainage 4, 14, 16, 19, 24, 30

Colorado River 29
cycle, water 5, 14, 31

dams 18, 19, 22-23, 26, 28, 29, 30
  Aswan 26
deltas 12, 13, 24, 26, 30, 31
deposition 5, 6, 7, 11, 17, 22, 30
discharge 14
distributaries 13, 26

energy 4, 20, 22, 23, 26
erosion 5, 6, 9, 10, 11, 12, 17, 22, 26, 30
estuaries 13
extraction (of river water) 20, 29, 30

fertilisers 26, 28, 30
flats, mud 13, 24
floods 5, 7, 11, 13, 14, 16-17, 18, 19, 21, 22, 24, 26, 30, 31
  flash 16, 19
flow, measuring river 14

gauges, stream 14, 19, 31

Gulf of Mexico 24

holes, sink 14, 30
Hurricane Katrina 24
hydroelectricity 22, 23, 26, 30, 31
hydrologists 8, 14, 15, 19, 30

industry 4, 20, 21, 24, 28, 29
irrigation 4, 20, 22, 26, 29

lakes 5, 8, 22, 24, 26, 29
  ox-bow 11, 17, 30, 31
levees 18, 19, 24
load 6, 7

marshes, salt 13, 24
meanders 10, 11, 12, 13, 17, 30, 31
micro-organisms 15, 20, 30
Mississippi River 24-25, 31
Missouri River 24
mouths (of rivers) 7, 12, 13, 24, 26, 29, 30

New Orleans 24

plains,
  coastal 12, 13
  flood 8, 10, 11, 16, 17, 18, 19, 30
pollutants 15, 28
pollution 15, 28
ports 21, 24, 26
prediction, flood 15, 16, 17

protection, flood 18-19, 28

quality, water 14, 15, 28

reservoirs 22, 23, 30
River Nile 26-27
River Ganges 12
River Rance 23
River Rhine 21
River Thames 18
river, stages of
  lower 8, 12-13, 17
  middle 8, 10-11, 17
  upper 8-9, 11, 17

sediment 6, 7, 10, 11, 12, 13, 15, 17, 22, 24, 26, 30
sources (of rivers) 4, 8, 30
springs 8, 30
supply, water 4, 15, 17, 18, 20, 22, 24, 28, 29
surges, storm 16, 24

Thames Barrier 18-19
tides 13, 18, 23, 30
transport 4, 18, 20, 21, 24, 26
transportation 6, 7, 30
tributaries 4, 12, 14, 24, 26, 30
turbulence 6, 7, 9, 10, 30

valleys 5, 8, 9, 10, 11, 22

warnings, flood 19, 31
waterfalls 9, 21
weathering, chemical 7, 30
weirs 21, 24